# THE PROFESSOR'S OUTLINE

## A SCREENPLAY

### Jason Holt

Anaphora Literary Press

Quanah, Texas

**Anaphora Literary Press**
1108 W 3rd Street
Quanah, TX 79252
https://anaphoraliterary.com

**Book design by Anna Faktorovich, Ph.D.**

Copyright © 2025 by Jason Holt

All rights reserved. No part of this book may be reproduced in any form or by any electronic or mechanical means, including information storage and retrieval systems, without permission in writing from Jason Holt. Writers are welcome to quote brief passages in their critical studies, as American copyright law dictates.

Printed in the United States of America, United Kingdom and in Australia on acid-free paper.

Published in 2025 by Anaphora Literary Press

The Professor's Outline: A Screenplay
Jason Holt—1st edition.

Library of Congress Control Number: 2025915553

**Library Cataloging Information**
Holt, Jason, 1971-, author.
    The professor's outline : A screenplay / Jason Holt
    56 p. ; 9 in.
    ISBN 978-1-68114-627-0 (softcover : alk. paper)
    ISBN 978-1-68114-628-7 (hardcover : alk. paper)
    Kindle (e-book)
1. Books—Literature & Fiction—Dramas & Plays—Contemporary.
2. Books—Arts & Photography—Performing Arts—Theater—Playwriting.
3. Books—Literature & Fiction—Dramas & Plays—Regional & Cultural—Canadian.
PN1997-1997.85: Drama: Motion Pictures: Screenplays
791.4372: Motion Pictures: Screenplays

# INTRODUCTION

Most published screenplays were first produced as films that achieved a certain level of distinction. But this screenplay has not yet been produced at all much less as a notable film. So why bother to publish it?

Here are some reasons. First, I believe it is a story worth telling in its original form, even the (pre)scriptive form of an envisioned film. The screenplay also suggests something more of a cinematic vision than would an artificial-feeling retelling as, say, a short novel, which is a type of literary expression I have already explored.[1] Last, along with having employed more conventional means of putting the screenplay into the hands of filmmakers, this printed format allows anyone who might be interested in the cinematic story to access it in some form without the necessity of production. And who knows? If this book falls into the right hands at the right time, its story may yet see the light of production.

Although I think the format is reader friendly, some abbreviations should be explained. For scene headings, "INT." indicates an interior location, "EXT." exterior. "O.S." indicates that a character is off screen, and "V.O." indicates voiceover. Other conventions, such as the use of capitals for scene headings and sounds, and italics for action and scene descriptions, should be intuitive enough on their face.

Finally, my gratitude to Dr. Anna Faktorovich at Anaphora Literary Press for supporting my work over the years, to my wife Megan for her ongoing love and support, to HGP for what was and what might have been, and to you for nothing less than picking up this book. I hope all of you find the effort worthwhile.

---

1    I refer to my trilogy of hard-to-find experimental novels: *Fragment of a Blues* (2001), *The Black Books Addiction* (2003), and *A Tangent at 3:15* (2009). A similar trilogy appears in this screenplay.

# **THE PROFESSOR'S OUTLINE**

FADE IN:

EXT. FOXBRIDGE CROSS – DAY

> We are in Foxbridge Cross, a college town typical of the east coast in Canada or New England. We see a quaint downtown, a mix of old and new buildings, residential streets, apartment blocks, and the campus of Arcana University, also a mix of older buildings, mostly brick, and more modern structures of steel and glass. The university boasts a modest enrolment of several thousand students and has an air of tradition, partly justified, somewhat complacent. It stands at the heart of yet apart from the surrounding town. Then we see, at close range, a police outline of a body with bloodstains at the head, as if the skull of the deceased had cracked open on the pavement.

INT. UNIVERSITY COLLEGE – DEPARTMENT MAILROOM – DAY

> Mail slots line one wall. A handful of PROFESSORS lounge on couches. Two seem paused mid conversation. Another is reading casually. SLOAT enters sporting a backpack and holding a banker's box in both hands. The professors seem not to register the newcomer as the two resume TALKING at a low, indiscernible volume. Sloat pauses at the threshold, taking in the scene. He crosses the room and finds his name on one of the mail slots. He smiles faintly. He taps his fingers on the bottom of the empty slot, sliding them over his name.

INT. UNIVERSITY COLLEGE – SLOAT'S OFFICE – DAY (LATER)

> A typical professor's office, complete with bookshelves—empty, at least for now—desk and chairs, an analog clock on otherwise bare walls, and a paned window. We hear the SOUND of a door being unlocked. The door swings open and SLOAT enters, with backpack and banker's box, shifting the latter to an empty bookcase. He removes a laptop from his backpack and opens it on the bare desk.

> *He consults a Post-it with username and password, types these in. He clicks on the email icon. We see a handful of emails, one from "Office of the President" with the subject line "New Faculty Reception". He clicks on the email.*

INT. ARCANA UNIVERSITY RECEPTION HALL – NIGHT

> *A wine and cheese event is in progress. PROFESSORS and ADMINSTRATORS stand scattered in the open or at tables alone or in small groups. For the most part there is a clear contrast between the older members of the group, fifty and up, who are more relaxed, more polished, and younger members in their late twenties to mid thirties. Among the former is the CHAIR, among the latter SLOAT. The Chair stands with a small GROUP, speaking inaudibly, lifting her chin at something in her field of vision. Sloat is standing alone near a table of hors d'oeuvres, holding a glass of white wine he sips absently. He is in his early thirties, not unhandsome, looking as if he is not quite in his element. His eyes fix on something approaching.*

ROMI (O.S.): And who might you be?

SLOAT: Uh, hi. John, John Sloat. I'm a new hire in M-DS.

> *ROMI, in her late thirties, put together, a statuesque blonde, looks like she understands something very important, a secret never to be revealed. She holds a glass of white wine.*

ROMI: Well, Dr. Sloat, you look like you need to be rescued. Tell me, what *is* meta-disciplinary studies? I've been asking for years, ever since the unit was founded. But nobody seems to know, not anyone in M-DS, anyway. I guess you're all trying to figure that out.

> *He nods. She considers him.*

ROMI (CONT'D): Call me Romi. Everyone does. I'm Chair over in English, so we're practically neighbors. I focus on English Renaissance. Elizabethan lit is my jam—well, my bread and butter.

SLOAT (*smiling at the joke*): Shakespeare?

ROMI: A little. Mostly Marlowe. And you? What's your thing?

SLOAT: I guess I'm a generalist looking for a focus. I haven't found the right foothold.

ROMI: Yes, you need a focus. Living in town?

SLOAT: Place on Eastwood, short term. Looking for something roomier, maybe a house, within walking distance.

ROMI: Well, when you get sorted you should host something yourself,

something a bit more intimate. This is no way to network.
SLOAT: I'm not here to network.
ROMI: Really?

INT. UNIVERSITY COLLEGE – CHAIR'S OFFICE – DAY
*A large corner office with expansive windows looking out on the quad and the town beyond. Two chairs sit before a broad desk with computer monitor and keyboard at one end and in- and out-boxes with official-looking documents at the other. Opposite is a love seat and two chairs around a coffee table. Above is an oversize abstract painting—black on white with splashes of gray. Something about the size of the painting and patches of black conveys menace. The door next to the painting stands open. Another, which is on another wall, stands closed. The CHAIR, wearing a tone-appropriate— yet eye-catching—pantsuit, sits at her desk looking at the monitor. Now and then she moves the mouse and clicks. SLOAT pokes his head in at the door.*
SLOAT: Am I early?
*The Chair looks up, then back at the screen. She remains seated.*
CHAIR: A little. (*Looking up again*) Please (*indicating the chairs*).
*Sloat gives a close-lipped smile as he enters and crosses to one of the chairs.*
CHAIR: Please.
*Sloat sits.*
SLOAT: So...
CHAIR: So, how was week one? Finding everything okay? Classes okay?
SLOAT: So far, so-kay.
CHAIR: Not sure about that one.
SLOAT: Me neither.
CHAIR: So, with new hires, I like to...
*She stops, looks at the monitor, clicks the mouse.*
CHAIR (CONT'D): You play poker, don't you? I seem to remember asking you during the interview process. But that was—what?—six-seven months ago? We have a regular game. Small stakes, no big deal. Someone just retired, and we're looking to complete our dirty half dozen. I assumed you'd want in.
*Sloat takes a beat.*
SLOAT: Sure, I've played.

CHAIR: Capital.
>*She types something quickly, hits return, then clicks the mouse.*

CHAIR (CONT'D): So, with new hires, I like to do an informal assessment, a week or so in, to ascertain the lie we're playing, what links need linking, what tees need crossing. I gather things have gone smoothly enough.

SLOAT: All things considered.

CHAIR: Good enough. (*Considers*) Have you met Jenson yet? Thought you might have, at the reception. He might be a good choice to show you the ropes—so you don't get tied up in knots.

SLOAT: Okay. I'll get in touch.

CHAIR: Other than that… (*frowns*)… there is the lingering matter of your research agenda. That was left as something of a promissory note during the interview process. Needless to say, it is absolutely vital that you define some sort of meta-disciplinary research agenda, and soon.

SLOAT: I know. I will, soon. I'm weighing a few possibilities.

CHAIR: Well, don't weigh them too long or too… carefully. You need a focus with "consensus significance"—I know, it's just a new buzzword—buzz*phrase*, really. But there you go. Okay?

>*With a perfunctory smile, the Chair stands up. Sloat stands up in turn.*

SLOAT: Okay.

EXT. CHAIR'S HOUSE – NIGHT

>*SLOAT approaches on foot, looking for a civic number. A few cars crowd the driveway and curbside. He walks under the carport to the side door. Lights are on inside, with a view of the empty kitchen. Muffled VOICES can be heard from another room, boisterous with the jovial tones of a small party in progress. Sloat knocks on the outer door, the inner door wide open. No response.*

INT. CHAIR'S HOUSE – KITCHEN – CONTINUOUS

>*SLOAT opens the door and steps in tentatively, closing the door behind him. The VOICES continue, less muffled. He wipes his feet on the mat.*

SLOAT: Hello?… *Hello!*

>*The voices drop for a moment.*

CHAIR (O.S.): Enter! *Willkommen*! Just follow the breadcrumbs.

SLOAT: Shoes on or off?

*Again, no response. The voices resume. Sloat waits, then removes his shoes and puts them neatly aside, hanging up his coat among the others. It takes him a moment to find a bare hook. He walks toward a doorway, the voices becoming louder as we discover that the doorway leads to a descending staircase. He begins the descent.*

INT. CHAIR'S HOUSE – BASEMENT – CONTINUOUS

*In a finished basement we see a poker table complete with green felt and built-in slots for chips at each place. At the table are the CHAIR, JENSON, and three other PLAYERS, finishing a hand. A couple of TV trays hold beverages and snacks. SLOAT enters, looks around at what is otherwise a typical man cave except that it belongs to the Chair.*

PLAYER 1 (*shaking his head*): I'm out.

PLAYER 2 (*tossing cards*): Out.

*Player 3 drops chips into the pot. Jenson, sitting to the right of the Chair, slides in his chips.*

CHAIR: Down and dirty.

*The game is seven-card stud. The Chair deals a card face down to Player 3, one to Jenson, and one to herself. She does not look at her last card. The others look at theirs.*

CHAIR: Pull up a chair. Make yourself at home. Some other hackneyed phrase.

SLOAT: Thanks again for the invite. You sure are well-stocked here. Still, you sure I shouldn't have brought anything?

CHAIR: Your twenty dollars will be quite sufficient. (*Tossing in chips*) Once more.

*Sloat finds a chair and drags it to the table, squeezing it in on Jenson's right. Player 3 folds. All eyes turn to Jenson, who looks at the Chair, smiles self-deprecatingly, and calls.*

JENSON: I've got to keep you honest, Madam Chair.

CHAIR: And so you should. I'm all blue, gentlemen.

*The chair reveals a flush and rakes in the pot.*

CHAIR (CONT'D): Don't be shy. We're all friends here, part of our little Arcana family.

*Sloat sits down, nods at the Chair. Jenson politely nods and smiles as if he is her proxy.*

JENSON: Twenty-dollar buy-in. Ante's 10, max bet is 50, three raises per round. Red's worth 10, white 25, blue 50.

> *Sloat hands a twenty-dollar bill to Jenson, the banker. Jenson hands over twenty red chips, thirty-two white, and twenty blue. Sloat arranges his chips neatly.*

SLOAT: No wild cards, I assume? Jacks or better, seven stud, hold 'em, that sort of thing?

JENSON: Also high-low, tombstones, cross, screw with "four-play", that sort of thing.

CHAIR (*shuffling*): Whose deal?

JENSON: Yours, Madam Chair.

> *Sloat gives Jenson a look. The Chair passes the cards for a cut.*

CHAIR: Ante up. Low Bogey.

> *Everyone antes but Sloat. The chair begins dealing seven-card stud.*

SLOAT (*to Jenson*): Low Bogey?

JENSON: Low spade in the hole takes half. I thought you knew how to play.

> *Sloat knits his brow, antes as if reluctantly.*

JENSON: Don't worry. You'll get it.

> *Later. A hand ends. Jenson wins a modest pot. Sloat has three chips left, one of each color.*

CHAIR: Gentlemen, our first Rubble pile.

> *Everyone except Sloat stands to give an OVATION. Sloat is a shade confused, but accepting. He tosses in his remaining chips.*

SLOAT: That's it for me.

JENSON: No, really?

SLOAT: Three buy-ins is enough.

> *Sloat rises. The Chair looks at her watch.*

CHAIR: I'm calling it. Time of death, 1 am. Until next time, gentlemen.

INT. SLOAT'S HOUSE – STUDY – DAY

> *A corner desk dominates the room, with a couch opposite and several bookcases against the walls and venetian blinds with slats turned horizontal. We can see autumn foliage through the slats. Moving boxes litter the room, one resting on the couch, some flapped open. Some books have been shelved. On the desk Sloat's laptop shows a word-processing document, which reads…*

JOHN SLOAT—RESEARCH OUTLINE

*As an Assistant Professor in meta-disciplinary studies, I plan to focus my research on [...]*

*Nothing follows the "on" except the cursor, flashing as though urgently. Beside the laptop are a pad of paper and pen, and beside these a pocketsize paperback book, novella-slim, with an abstract gray cover: "Where Wise Men Never Go" by "Jonas Thol". SLOAT stands amidst the disorder, surveying the terrain. He grabs the pen and pad of paper. He shifts the box from the couch to make room. He stretches himself long on the couch, feet sticking over the armrest. He consults the pad, pen poised. The pad, with a list of names, reads...*

> ROMI –
> JENSON – ?
> RAMSAY – ✓
> BEARDSLEY – ✓
> STANLEY –
> NORRIS – ✓
> HOLT – X
> COHEN –

*The pen wavers, then puts an "X" beside "Romi". Sloat EXHALES through his nose. The pen wavers, puts a question mark beside "Stanley", a check mark beside "Cohen". Sloat's head, figuring the permutations, oscillates side to side, then stops. He purses his lips, nods.*

INT. SLOAT'S HOUSE – BATHROOM – DAY

*SLOAT is in the shower rubbing shampoo into his hair. The showerhead HISSES. He sticks his head under the showerhead to rinse off. He lathers his face for a wet shave. He rinses a razor, his face fully lathered, then begins to shave, starting under his nose, and holding a travel mirror in his left hand. He rinses his face, shave complete, under the showerhead. He steps back and shakes the water from his hair. He squints at the mirror again, retrieves the razor, and catches a few stray whiskers just below his nostrils. He puts the razor down, picks up soap, starts working it vigorously into a lather. He steps, lathered head to toe, under the showerhead. He shakes water from his hair, then grabs the soap again and works it over his undercarriage a second time. Later. He stands at the bathroom sink wearing a towel and wipes fog from the mirror, looking at his face in three-quarter views. He applies deodorant after sniffing it. He finger-brushes his hair into presentable shape.*

INT. SLOAT'S HOUSE – BEDROOM – DAY (LATER)

*SLOAT, in underwear and tank top, studies himself in a full-length mirror. Later. He stands in a similar position in front of the mirror in slacks and a collared shirt. There is a sportscoat on the bed beside him. He touches up his hair, then considers the sportscoat.*

INT. SLOAT'S HOUSE – LIVING/DINING ROOM – DAY (LATER)

*The room is clean and tidy: a four-seat dining-room set in the dining area, with a doorway to a galley kitchen, an adjoining spacious living room with an entertainment center along one wall, a filled bookcase opposite. SLOAT, in slacks and collared shirt—no sportscoat—stands looking at a sideboard with all the paraphernalia for a cocktail party perfectly arranged: stainless steel shaker, cocktail glasses, ice bucket, garnishes, bottles of vodka, gin, and vermouth, and wooden barbecue skewers cut into swizzle sticks. Behind him, various snacks have been arranged on the dining room table. He steps back, then spreads his hands, framing the scene, then holds for a moment. He gives a slight smile and nod. He half turns, stops, then returns to the sideboard, tilting his head.*

SLOAT: Those skewers will have to do.

*He SIGHS, glancing off at a wall clock, which shows 7:40.*

SLOAT: Twenty minutes. Any time now.

*He exits down the corridor.*

INT. SLOAT'S HOUSE – BATHROOM – DAY (LATER)

*SLOAT flushes the toilet, washes and dries his hands. He checks his watch, then looks at himself in the mirror. He touches up his hair, then breathes deeply and slowly, in through the nose, out through the mouth. He exits, leaving the bathroom door open.*

INT. SLOAT'S HOUSE – LIVING/DINING ROOM –

CONTINUOUS

> SLOAT *enters and sits—almost perching—on the couch, his foot oscillating. He looks out the window, then grabs the TV remote, turns it on, then snaps it off again, staring into space. Later. Sloat is sitting in the same position. The wall clock shows 8:12. The summer daylight is dimming somewhat. He looks at his watch, then the wall clock, and again out the window.*

SLOAT: Fashionably late, I suppose. Well…

> *He rises, goes over to the window, and looks out, craning his neck. The front walkway is empty. Back to living/dining room. He exits down the corridor again, returning after a few seconds holding* WHERE WISE MEN NEVER GO, *which he drops onto the coffee table. He exits again, this time into the galley kitchen. We hear the CRACK and FIZZ of a carbonated can opening. He returns with a can of soda water, sitting down once more. He picks up the book, scans the back cover quickly, takes a sip of soda. He looks once more—almost in passing—to the window. He begins to read.*

INT. SLOAT'S HOUSE – LIVING/DINING ROOM – NIGHT (LATER)

> *The same view, but darkness has fallen. The wall clock shows almost 9:00. Sloat is a good way into the book, maybe 20–25 pages. He does not look at the window or check the time again. He reaches for the soda can, finds it empty, leaving it and the book on the coffee table as he rises. He walks over to the sideboard and begins to make himself a martini: CLATTERING ice in the shaker, measuring vodka and adding a drop of vermouth. The SHAKING is slow and regular, seeming to go on longer than necessary.*

INT. ROMI'S HOUSE – BEDROOM – DAY

> *Two years later. We are in a well-curated master bedroom with a king-size bed, many white and off-white surfaces. Sunlight streams in through the window.* SLOAT *and* ROMI *are in bed. He lies on his back with head tilted and arm extended toward her. She lies turned away. All we see of her is a tangled mass of blonde hair above the duvet. He lies in sunlight, she in shade. Sloat squints awake, reaches for Romi, but stops short of touching, then EXHALES. He sits up, feet on the floor, YAWNS, and stretches. Then he looks at the bedside clock, breathes again and stands. He looks*

at Romi, tightens his mouth, and walks into the ensuite bathroom on her side of the bed, closing the door softly behind him.

INT. ROMI'S HOUSE – KITCHEN – DAY (LATER)

*The kitchen is spacious, well-appointed, and looks new or newly renovated. SLOAT, dressed in business casual slacks and shirt, stands at the counter, blending a breakfast smoothie. The BLENDING is notably loud and grindy. He stops blending and puts the covered container in the fridge, then removes bags of blueberries and raspberries from the freezer. He brings the bags to the stove, where a shallow pot of oatmeal is simmer-bubbling. He stirs the pot vigorously, as if the oatmeal is sticking to the bottom. He stirs in blueberries straight from the bag, then adds raspberries by squeezing each into fragments between his thumb and index finger. He covers the pot, turns off the stove, and replaces the bags in the freezer. Sloat now appears tight, a little on edge. He moves over to the coffeemaker, still brewing, pouring himself a cup. He adds milk and takes a swallow, his face softening. Coffee cup in hand, he walks over to the window and looks out, taking another sip.*

INT. ROMI'S HOUSE – TV ROOM – DAY (LATER)

*SLOAT is sitting on the couch with a bowl of oatmeal in his lap, his coffee cup at his elbow. He faces a massive flatscreen TV, which remains off. Light comes in through an expansive side window. Opposite there is an adjoining foyer with winter coats and boots. With one hand, he splays open a slim black book entitled "The Next Thing" by "Jonas Thol". With the other he sets aside the bowl and grabs the coffee cup. Before taking a sip, he speaks…*

SLOAT: Oh, so good. Thol, you devil. How did I not see that before?

*He sips, puts down the cup, and jots down something in a notebook. He sips again, notices the time on his watch, then puts the book and notebook in his backpack. He rises, leaves the backpack on the couch as he busses bowl and cup, exiting. Later, Sloat is in the foyer with backpack and travel mug, bundling up for winter weather.*

EXT. ROMI'S HOUSE – DRIVEWAY – CONTINUOUS

*It is winter. There is snow but it is not recent, none on the streets, sidewalks, driveways, or vehicles. There are two cars in the drive, one facing in, midrange, gleaming, the other facing out, economy, smudged with winter grime. SLOAT emerges from the front door and locks it with a key on his key chain. He approaches the grimy car, opens the door, then sets the backpack on the passenger seat and the travel mug in the cupholder before getting in. We hear SOUNDS of the ignition turning over not the first time, but the second. The car pulls out of the driveway into the wider streets of an upper-middle-class neighborhood, turning left, then right. The car turns onto a highway onramp.*

INT. SLOAT'S CAR – DAY (LATER)
*SLOAT, his coat unzipped, sits in the driver's seat. His face is somewhat tense as he checks his mirrors to merge. Then his face softens. He takes a sip of coffee, settling in for the drive. After a while, his neutral expression shades concerned, as if asking himself a question, then allowing himself the slight smile of an answer.*
ROMI (V.O.): Have dinner with me.

FLASHBACK: PUB – NIGHT
*ROMI and SLOAT are sitting in a booth. They look at each other across the table. A SERVER drops menus and leaves.*
SLOAT: I'm really glad you asked me to dinner. My socializing has been kind of sporadic. A slow start is one thing, but I thought I'd hit my stride by now. Not that I have a ton of free time, with all new preps this term and next.
ROMI: Sorry I couldn't make the cocktail party. How did it go?
SLOAT (*looking away*): It went.
   *Beat.*
ROMI: What?
SLOAT: Just remembering something my father said. I never made friends easily, always had trouble connecting. In high school, when it got really bad, dad told me to have patience. There'd be people in university to connect with. When I was in university, he said wait till grad school.
ROMI: And now?
SLOAT: He passed away last year. He was my best friend.
ROMI: Maybe we can be friends. I'd like that.
SLOAT (*shy*): Me too. (*Looking around*) I like this place. I thought you'd pick something more upscale. Going gentle on the modest wallet

of the junior prof?
ROMI (*waving it off*): No, this is on me. I asked *you* to dinner, after all.
   *The server returns.*
SERVER: Are you ready?
ROMI (*to Sloat*): Oh, I'm ready. Are you?
END FLASHBACK

   *Sloat takes an offramp toward a gas station sign.*

EXT. GAS STATION – DAY (LATER)
   SLOAT *stands beside his car at a pump. He taps his credit card, selects a grade, inserts the nozzle, and starts to pump gas. Lifting his head, he sees a* COUPLE *at another pump, the woman replacing the nozzle and replacing the cap, the man returning with coffee and snacks. Their movements are complementary and accented by an exchange of smiles. We hear the* SOUND (O.S.) *of a key opening a lock.*
ROMI (V.O.): I think you'd better come in.

FLASHBACK: INT. ROMI'S HOUSE – FOYER – NIGHT
   ROMI *opens the door and steps in, taking off her coat and turning to* SLOAT, *who follows her in and closes the door.*
ROMI: I can't thank you enough for the drive.
SLOAT: Don't give it thought. I was going to come in anyway. Thought I might catch something at the megaplex. I hear *Namaste, Motherfucker* is well worth it.
ROMI: How about some coffee, by way of thanking you? Give me your coat.
SLOAT (*checking his watch*): Thanks. Why not?

FLASHBACK (CONT'D): INT. ROMI'S HOUSE – KITCHEN – NIGHT (LATER)
   ROMI *stands frowning at the coffeemaker, while* SLOAT *looks at her. Beat. She turns toward him, suddenly animated.*
ROMI: Ooh, I'll make martinis! Vodka?
SLOAT (*hesitant*): Ooh…
ROMI: One isn't going to hurt, is it?
SLOAT: I guess not.

FLASHBACK (CONT'D): INT. ROMI'S HOUSE – TV ROOM – NIGHT (LATER)
> ROMI and SLOAT are sitting at a close but still friendly distance on the couch. Soft MUSIC plays. Romi is holding an empty martini glass. Sloat's, half full, rests on the coffee table.

ROMI: You should stay.

SLOAT: Do think we should? I mean, you're an administrator, and I'm...

ROMI: In no shape to drive.

SLOAT: But... how will it look? Shouldn't we worry about appearances?

ROMI (*standing*): It will look like it is.

> She takes a few steps as if to leave, then stops, looking back at him over her shoulder.

ROMI: Come on, Johnny.

END FLASHBACK

> Sloat finishes filling up. He removes the nozzle, clicks the gas cap closed, then closes the flap and replaces the nozzle. He gets back in the car and drives off toward the onramp.

INT. SLOAT'S CAR – DAY (LATER)
> SLOAT bears off the highway at another offramp. He turns right onto a winding road. We see farmland, a scattering of trees, some houses along the road. Snow is everywhere except for the bare road.

EXT. FOXBRIDGE CROSS – MAIN STREET – DAY (LATER)
> SLOAT'S CAR drives past a large sign reading "Welcome to Foxbridge Cross – Home of Arcana University". Later. A spacious parking lot—for a small town—at the edge of town. About half the spaces are occupied. The car turns into the lot, slides into a space and pulls forward into the next, which is also empty. SLOAT gets out. He leaves travel mug and backpack inside and zips up his coat. As he walks toward downtown along the sidewalk he hunches shoulders, bracing himself against the winter wind.

FLASHBACK: ROMI'S HOUSE – TV ROOM – DAY
> ROMI is lounging on the couch, absently watching TV. We hear the SOUND of a key unlocking the front door. SLOAT enters by

the front door, holding his backpack. He closes and locks the door, then kicks off his shoes, putting down the backpack and shrugging off his jacket.

SLOAT: Hey you. What a day. You wouldn't believe what the Chair said about my abstract.

*She glares at him.*

ROMI: I'm *watching* this.

*He puts his hands up.*

SLOAT: Sorry.

*She widens eyes at him, her mouth corners pulling back. He raises his hands even higher, EXHALES dropping them, then exits into the kitchen.*

FLASHBACK (CONT'D): ROMI'S HOUSE – KITCHEN – NIGHT

*SLOAT is making supper, stir fry SIZZLING on the stove. He stirs the pan, fluffs the rice in a pot. We hear the SLAM of a door.*

SLOAT: Hey-oh! In here!

*ROMI enters, approaches the counter. Still attending to the stove, he pours a glass of white wine and hands it to her. As he does so, he speaks.*

SLOAT: I got everything on the list. But they didn't have the salad. I got romaine hearts instead. Dinner is pretty much ready.

ROMI: Let me decompress, okay? I *just* got home. Jesus.

*She gulps half the wine, closing her eyes, then turns and leaves, glass in hand. He watches her leave.*

SLOAT: Okay.

*He stirs the pan once more, then covers it, and turns off the heat. After a beat, he looks up at the empty doorway, goes over to the cupboard for a shallow plate, which he brings back to the stove.*

FLASHBACK (CONT'D): INT. ROMI'S HOUSE – BEDROOM – NIGHT

*ROMI is reading in bed. We hear SOUNDS of teeth-brushing from the ensuite. SLOAT enters from the ensuite in sleep attire. He walks around to the other side of the bed and slips under the covers. He looks at her.*

SLOAT: Hey.

*He shifts closer and begins to rub her shoulders. She ignores him.*

*Still rubbing her shoulders, he kisses her neck.*
SLOAT: Hey.
*She widens eyes at him.*
SLOAT (*inviting*): It's Saturday night.
*She looks away.*
ROMI (*facetious*): Huh, *Saturday night.*
FLASHBACK ENDS

*Sloat, walking, now in the heart of downtown, bristles at another gust of wind. He turns the corner, crosses the street, and approaches a knot of winter-bundled STRIKERS gathered to take a picket shift. In the front window of the building behind them is a sign reading "AFA Headquarters". We see hand-held union signs and sandwich boards: "AFA", "Arcana Faculty Care", "Education Matters", etc. Sloat navigates through the cluster and enters the building.*

EXT. FOXBRIDGE CROSS – MAIN STREET – DAY (LATER)
*We are on a stretch sidewalk of several hundred yards in front of a large-lettered sign, "Arcana University", behind which a quad slopes uphill to an imposing administration building. PICKETERS with union signs and sandwich boards walk back and forth along the sidewalk, some in single-file lines, others in tandem walking abreast, the odd lone wolf. Snow hems them in on either side. SLOAT and JENSON are among the strikers, walking together in tandem. Sloat is wearing an "AFA" sandwich board while Jenson holds an "Education Matters" sign on his shoulder.*
JENSON: How long have we been at it?
SLOAT (*checking his watch*): Twenty minutes to go—a little more.
JENSON: Jesus. Over an hour and a half of this.
SLOAT: It's not so bad. Plus, don't you already have tenure? That's some compensation.
JENSON: No. Up this year. But no worries. I've published. The Chair likes me. Once you get renewed, that's what you'll have to worry about.
SLOAT: How much longer do you think this will last?
JENSON: Oh, two-three weeks. They have to save enough to pay for whatever they end up giving us, something anyway. Nobody wins, but everybody saves face. At least we don't have to prep for a month or so. I need a break from research too.

SLOAT: Did I tell you they accepted my abstract? Fly out tomorrow. The warm weather alone will make it worthwhile, though I gather it's not a dry heat.
JENSON: Uh, you do know we're supposed to withhold our work during a strike, right? That includes conferencing.
SLOAT (*not convinced*): I need to get something into shape for publication.
JENSON: I guess so.
> *Sloat falls back to make room for a group of strikers passing the other way. Then he catches back up.*

JENSON (CONT'D): So, what's it like sleeping with the enemy?
> *Sloat stops in his tracks and looks hard at Jenson. Jenson takes another two steps, stops, and turns.*

JENSON (CONT'D): What?

INT. CONFERENCE ROOM – THE CITY – DAY
> *It is a typical conference room with chairs arranged in two sections with an aisle in the middle. A dozen PEOPLE are sitting in the audience, including DEVYN in the back row, easy to miss despite her appropriate but offbeat attire, QUESTIONER 1 in the front row, and QUESTIONER 2 on the aisle halfway down. Everyone is wearing conference badges. Some attendees are cradling coffee cups. Other cups are set on the floor. At the front stands SLOAT behind a lectern with his open laptop and notes. Behind him is a screen showing a title slide that reads "Jonas Thol: A New Direction in Writing" with "Dr. John Sloat" below. The slide has Arcana University branding. All eyes turn to the front, waiting but not particularly expectant. Sloat checks his watch, then touches his notes. As Sloat begins to speak, several LATECOMERS enter. They and a few others find seats.*

SLOAT (*projecting*): I suppose we should begin. Thank you all for coming this afternoon, and for the opportunity to speak to you on a writer of remarkable importance—Jonas Thol—whose work deserves a central place not only on our shelves, but also in meta-disciplinary studies. After all, as dedicated scholars in M-DS, we are still trying to figure out what we are, to carve out that special place that isn't quite—but isn't quite *not*—literary studies or philosophy. I will argue that Thol's trilogy of experimental novels provides the means for us to do just that. Without further ado, I'd like to begin with a close, but somewhat idiosyncratic, reading of Thol's first experimental novel.

> *Sloat advances to the next slide, titled "The First Book", a cover image of* Where Wise Men Never Go—*gray, abstract—on the right and the following bullet points on the left:*

> - First in the "ought" trilogy
> - New kind of writing
> - Draws on yet transcends
>   - Existentialist worldview
>   - New novel minimalism
>   - Poetic technique, rhythm

SLOAT (CONT'D): My research is predicated on the notion that aesthetic reward is absolutely vital for the kind of work we do in M-DS…

> *Later. Sloat is still standing at the lectern. A slide shows a gray circle on the left, a yin-yang symbol on the right, in between an arrow pointing right.*

SLOAT: …Which means, now that we have passed through gray and black and have arrived finally at white—a white jacket with black underneath—Thol prompts us to consider the progressive kinship between Western perspectives such as Stoicism and Existentialism and Asian perspectives such as Daoism and some elements of Buddhism. And with that… (*advancing to a blank slide*) I thank you.

> *APPLAUSE comes a little late and a little weak, almost a grudging courtesy. Sloat EXHALES.*

SLOAT (CONT'D): Any questions?

> *Three less than enthusiastic hands go up, including those of Questioner 1 and Questioner 2. Sloat nods at Questioner 1 and opens an inviting palm. The other two questioners' hands fall.*

QUESTIONER 1 (*smiling paternally*): Let me get my thoughts together here. I understand that you have an appreciation for this—what's his name?—Thol. Okay, but I'm not satisfied that *I* myself have any reason to bother. I mean, you readily admit, there's simply no consensus significance here. The work *I'm* interested in—that we *all* should be interested in in M-DS—is work that already *has* consensus significance. I'm simply not convinced by your argument.

SLOAT (*with open palms*): Two things. First, if what I've said doesn't pique your interest, even a little, in Thol's work, in its potential significance, then maybe it's not for you—that's fine. But that doesn't mean the work doesn't hold great promise for meta-disciplinary studies—as I've argued. The novels don't have consensus significance—yet. How could they? Obscure as they are, they nonetheless *deserve* to be considered worthy candidates. M-DS needs to grow and evolve in establishing its own legitimacy if it is to thrive at all.

> *Questioner 1 frowns, shaking his head. The other two hands are raised again. Sloat looks at Questioner 2.*

SLOAT: Yes?

QUESTIONER 2: I'm worried about your response to the previous question. Seems to me there's no place in M-DS for mere preference, aesthetic response, or anything but cultural presence, and what is that but cultural prominence? Preferential and aesthetic matters will be irrelevant or else should be tailored by the need to defend and define disciplinary *objectives*, not "subjectives". I can't see how any of this (*waves hand at screen*) helps at all.

> *Sloat looks down, deflated for a moment, then looks up.*

SLOAT: Let me come at this from another angle.

INT. COFFEESHOP – THE CITY – NIGHT (LATER)

> *A typical urban coffeeshop: tables and low chairs, bars and barstools at high windows, a scattering of PATRONS, most sitting alone with one or two twosomes. SLOAT stands at the counter, looking at the chalkboard behind a BARISTA, whose patience is wearing thin at the end of a long shift.*

SLOAT: For here, please, a 12-ounce 1% misto.

> *He EXHALES, tapping fingers on the counter.*

BARISTA: Is that for here?

> *He smiles, lips closed.*

SLOAT: Please.

> *Later. Sloat is sitting at a table near the wall, writing in a pocket notebook. He pauses, looks off for a moment, then finishes writing and closes the notebook. He is about to sip his coffee when he is stopped by…*

DEVYN (O.S.): Excuse me.

> *DEVYN perches on a barstool at the window, turned to address him. She is wearing a conference badge. She is brunette, mid-thirties, and exudes a kind of exuberant warmth. She gives the impression of living on hope, a not yet desperate hope that the right alchemy at the right time would make life precious, truly extraor-*

*dinary.*
DEVYN (CONT'D): I didn't want to interrupt.
> *He lifts his hands, palms open, then chins at her badge.*

SLOAT: Enjoying the conference?
DEVYN: Yes, very much.
> *Devyn notices the badge, smiles and shrugs, rolling eyes at herself, takes it off, and tucks it away.*

SLOAT: You presenting?
DEVYN: No, not here. Not yet.
SLOAT: You were at my talk, weren't you? I thought you looked familiar.
> *She nods.*

DEVYN: To be honest, I'm not here for the conference, not the whole thing. I came to see you. Your abstract was *so* intriguing.
SLOAT: On the great, unsung Jonas Thol? You know his work? Don't tell me you're a fan.
DEVYN: I am. I really am. The writing is so… *different*, you know? Such a unique voice.
SLOAT: Isn't it? I'm trying to make the case… well, of course you know. Which stuff have you read?
DEVYN: Everything, the whole—what did you call it?—ought trilogy. It really speaks to me. It resonates, you know?
SLOAT: I love work like that. Fits your psyche like a glove, almost as if you wrote it yourself.
> *She smiles.*

DEVYN: I know what you mean.

EXT. SIDEWALK – THE CITY – NIGHT (LATER)
> *SLOAT and DEVYN meander along the sidewalk, eyes down, smiling. Their strides are complementary—but not always in sync.*

SLOAT: How'd you get introduced to Thol?
DEVYN: Ooh, hard to say. I honestly can't remember. You?
SLOAT: A used bookstore, totally random, a place called Odd Books. Do you know Foxbridge Cross?
DEVYN: I do. I'm a librarian at Arcana.
SLOAT: You're kidding. We're both in the same building. Small world.
DEVYN: Not too small. You know, I worked part time at Odd Books while doing my masters.
> *They stop at an intersection waiting for the light. Sloat looks both*

*ways for cross traffic. There is none. Devyn's focus is entirely local—their shared bubble. They walk on when the light changes.*

SLOAT: I love having the café right in the building. But don't you hate that it closes so early on Fridays? I mean, 2 o'clock? Don't they know we're academics?

DEVYN: I go downtown for coffee every Friday afternoon. If I don't, I'm flat on the pavement.

SLOAT: Me too.

*He looks at her.*

SLOAT (CONT'D): We must have crossed paths at some point.

*She looks at him.*

DEVYN: We were bound to.

*She looks away.*

DEVYN (CONT'D): But I've seen you at checkout a few times, once or twice in the stacks. You like hard copies, don't you? I echo that sentiment, if you'll allow it.

SLOAT: I'll allow it.

*She looks up, gestures.*

DEVYN: This is my hotel.

SLOAT: Mine too.

*She lifts an eyebrow.*

DEVYN: Well, then.

SLOAT: Look, listen, I live with someone.

DEVYN: I know—I know what this is. I know what I am.

INT. DEVYN'S APARTMENT – DAY

*A cozy studio apartment with a window letting in a lot of natural light and facing a public park. In one corner the couch faces a small flatscreen TV. Behind the couch is a dining nook abutting on the kitchen area, with a double bed near the wall bathed in light from the window. DEVYN and SLOAT are lying in bed, Sloat on his back with face turned away. Devyn is a mass of dark hair above the covers. Devyn stirs, smiling at Sloat even before her eyes open, then smiles more when her eyes do open. She slides over, gently turns his face toward her, then kisses him awake.*

DEVYN: Good morning, you. Happy six-month anniversary.

SLOAT (*yawning*): Is it six months already?

*He kisses her.*

SLOAT (CONT'D): Sorry, I didn't get you anything.

DEVYN: You're the worst. No, you're mine, for the *whole* weekend.
> *She strokes his chest.*

DEVYN (CONT'D): That's all I need—I'll make us breakfast.
> *She gets up, throws on a robe. He GROANS and stretches.*

SLOAT: You're the best.
> *Later. Devyn and Sloat, still in sleepwear and robes, lounge on the couch, watching TV. The SOUND from the TV is low and generic. On the coffee table are two coffee cups, Devyn's plate with toast fragments and fork. Sloat finishes his omelet, tables his plate, and takes a sip of coffee.*

SLOAT: Mmm. So good. I'm not usually an omelet guy. Love the veg.

DEVYN: It's a Devyn omelet. My own twist on a classic.

SLOAT: What's the twist? It's something I can't quite put my finger on. Some kind of spice, maybe?

DEVYN: It's a secret. I'll never tell.
> *He embraces her.*

SLOAT: Tell me. Perhaps I can persuade you.
> *She kisses him upward.*

DEVYN: Perhaps. You'll just have to wait and see.
> *They lean away from each other, still smiling, a natural respite. Devyn picks up the remote control, presses a button, then another at regular intervals.*

DEVYN (CONT'D): Let's see whether the programing gods are smiling on us.
> *She continues pressing the remote, pauses.*

DEVYN (CONT'D): Oh, tonight they're showing *Namaste, Motherfucker*. That sounds terrible. We *have* to watch it.

SLOAT: Absolutely. Actually, I've been wanting to see it for some time. I'll make popcorn.

DEVYN: Deal.

EXT. FOXBRIDGE CROSS – PARK – DAY (LATER)
> *A public park with walking paths winding through expanses of green lawns and into forested areas. Picnic tables and benches are situated on the grass near a small beach that borders on a large swimming pond. It is a cloudless summer day drenched in sunlight. There are many PEOPLE enjoying the park: some swimmers, outnumbered by sunbathers, teens playing frisbee, and on the walking paths most walking, some joggers and cyclists. SLOAT*

*and DEVYN, in shorts and summer shirts, are walking along a sunlit path.*

SLOAT: I finally heard back from the *Journal of Meta-Disciplinary Studies* about my paper. It's a revise and resubmit. Should take me a week or two to work through the comments.

DEVYN: How were the comments?

SLOAT: Mixed, as you'd expect. Not sure how to reply to the more serious ones—complaints, really. You know, the old "I'm interested in other things" kind of complaint.

*Beat.*

SLOAT (CONT'D): Oh, I forgot to tell you. I think I have a lead on Thol's identity. You know how I think "Jonas Thol" is most likely a pseudonym? You're with me on that, right?

DEVYN: I guess so.

SLOAT: Well, I don't know why I didn't think of it before, but on the ISBN page—of each book—it says the publisher is Minerva's Perch, and it's the same printer as well. So also on my to-do list is seeing what I can dig up there.

DEVYN: Maybe you need a break, and more than just a weekend with me.

*Beat.*

SLOAT: I was thinking of adding another physical activity to my routine, especially given the commute, but I hadn't given it much thought.

*She embraces him, then lets go.*

DEVYN: Aren't you getting enough physical activity already? I know. Why not martial arts? I know someone who teaches evening classes.

SLOAT: In…?

DEVYN: I think it's called jitsu do. It's supposed to be like ai jitsu with some ju kwon techniques—a blend of striking and grappling. Kind of like MMA, but more traditional.

SLOAT: You're so knowledgeable—and intuitive. I've always wanted to try martial arts.

DEVYN: I'm sure you can take a free trial class. See whether you take to it.

*He nods.*

INT. DEVYN'S APARTMENT – NIGHT (LATER)

*DEVYN and SLOAT are standing in the kitchen area. There is a large pot with a long handle on the largest burner. The overhead stove light is on. Beside the stove on the counter various items are arrayed, including a sizeable stainless-steel bowl, a jar of coconut oil, a mason jar filled with unpopped popcorn, measuring cups (quarter-cup and one-cup), a saltshaker, and a butter knife. Devyn watches while Sloat brims the one-cup measure with popcorn kernels. He then uses the butter knife to pack coconut oil—which is solid—into the quarter-cup measure, levelling it at the top.*

SLOAT: There we go.
*He frames the scene with his hands.*
SLOAT (CONT'D): I think we're there: pot… check, bowl… check, popcorn… check, oil… check, salt… check. I think we're set.
DEVYN: You're the popcorn wrangler. Oh, drinks. I'm thinking wine.
SLOAT: Okay, you're the sommelier. What do you recommend?
*She hunts for a bottle.*
DEVYN: I'm thinking a cabernet. I know you like "sauvignon" as a prefix, but I'm hoping to convert you to reds.
*She displays a bottle.*
SLOAT: Okay.
DEVYN: I'm going to let this breathe. Go ahead. I'm watching.
*She fishes a waiter's corkscrew out of a drawer, paying attention to Sloat's procedure. Sloat describes each key step in the process as he performs it.*
SLOAT: Okay. Burner on high. Fan on. Coconut oil.
*He scrapes the oil into the pot.*
SLOAT (CONT'D): Add three kernels.
*He drops in the kernels.*
SLOAT (CONT'D): When these pop, we add the rest, cover, and shake.
*Later. They are drinking wine. We hear a soft, steady HISS from the stove, followed by three discernible POPS. Sloat puts down his glass, checks his watch. He points at the glass.*
SLOAT: This is really good. I'm impressed.
*He puts the kernels in, covers the pot, and gives it a shake, saying…*
SLOAT (CONT'D): We add the popcorn. Cover. Shake back and forth now and then, until the popping really gets going. Put the bowl and salt here.
*She complies, then hands him his glass.*
SLOAT (CONT'D): I'm really looking forward to this movie.
*He hugs her.*

SLOAT (CONT'D): And there's no one I'd rather see it with.
DEVYN: I didn't know this was a Johnny Chen film. He's a legend. Maybe the title isn't such a joke as I thought.
SLOAT: I've been a huge Johnny Chen fan since I was a kid. I think we're in for a treat. I hope so. He is getting on, but martial artists sometimes keep their chops until they get really old.

> *We hear POPS from the stove, one at first, then a few, then building to a chaotic frenzy. Sloat again describes each key step in the procedure as he performs it.*

SLOAT (CONT'D): Keep shaking, more regularly now. Hold the lid in place. When the volume builds, put about half into the bowl, like so. A little salt, and back to shaking. Repeat when the volume builds again. More salt. Heat off as the pops slow down, but keep shaking. When the pops stop, dump in the rest, like so. Salt. Fan off. Then mix, like so. There's a knack to it.

> *He flips the popcorn up—from the back of the bowl—and catches it at the front. He repeats this twice more. He presents the bowl.*

SLOAT (CONT'D): Et voilà!

> *She takes a big handful.*

DEVYN (*munching*): Mmm, so good. I think we're ready. Well, not quite.

> *While she refills their glasses, he checks his watch.*

SLOAT: Perfect.

> *Later. They are sitting on the couch, popcorn between them and wine glasses on the coffee table. Their faces are aglow, reflecting light from the TV.*

DEVYN: *Namaste, Motherfucker*. Bring it on.

> *They smile at each other. She raises her glass.*

DEVYN (CONT'D): To Johnny Chen.
SLOAT: To Johnny Chen.

> *They toast.*

MONTAGE OF MOVIE-WATCHING:

> *We see DEVYN and SLOAT on the couch, their eyes and bodies in parallel while watching, bathed in the glow from the TV. They flinch together—then look at each other in sheer delight. They alternate grabbing handfuls of popcorn without having to look down. They watch the screen with half-full wine glasses in hand, making simultaneous sour faces, half turning away and jostling*

*each other—but without spilling the wine. She throws popcorn at him, just one kernel, hitting him in the face. He throws one at her—but, pushing her lips out like Bruce Lee, she bats it away with the back of a flat hand like a martial artist. They laugh, then turn back to the screen, sinking comfortably into the couch.*

END OF MONTAGE

*Later. They are on the couch, the TV glow still on their faces, the sound muted. She turns off the TV, killing the glow. She turns to him.*

DEVYN: That was so great. Thanks for suggesting it.

SLOAT: Yeah, it was. Thank *you* for being so… amenable.

DEVYN: Don't mention it, although…

*She throws a leg over, straddling him, her hands sliding to his shoulders, then the back of his neck.*

DEVYN (CONT'D): …I take it I'm not the only one here who's… amenable.

*She smiles. He lifts his face to hers. She tilts her head down to kiss him, at first with closed lips, then open and more insistent, her hips shifting. He GROANS in surrender. Closeup of her lips smiling in response.*

MONTAGE OF LOVEMAKING:

*SLOAT lies face-up on the bed, his hands on her hips as DEVYN sits upright astride him. They are half covered by a draping top sheet, some shade of taupe. ROMANTIC MUSIC plays. No other sounds are audible. He slides his hands from her hips to lie palms up beside his head, almost an invitation. She leans forward to kiss him. Her right hand covers his left, their palms clasped, fingers entwined. Against the bottom sheet, their clasped hands move back and forth in a steady rhythm. His right hand now covers her left, fingers entwined and palms together as before, only with parties switched. The rhythmic motion continues. His right hand, palm down as before, now covers the back of her right hand, their fingers entwined. The rhythmic movement continues, yet more insistently. The hands convulse even tighter together, then relax in sync. The music fades.*

END OF MONTAGE

*Later. Devyn and Sloat are lounging in bed together, their joint afterglow complemented by a light on the nightstand. She takes a sip from a water glass, then hands it to him. He drinks, then holds the glass in his lap.*

SLOAT: Thanks. That was something.

DEVYN: No, that was something else.

*Beat.*

SLOAT: Did you get that from Thol? *The Next Thing*?

*She knits her brow, eyes moving off.*

DEVYN: I guess I did.

*She takes a beat, then eyes him directly.*

DEVYN (CONT'D): But isn't it the third book? Isn't it from *Up Against Beyond*?

SLOAT: I'm pretty sure it's the second book. I quoted that line in my paper.

DEVYN: I'm sure you're right.

*They both smile, sinking deeper into the bed, their eyes losing focus for a moment.*

DEVYN (CONT'D): You know, something in that movie tonight made me think of *Eyes Wide Shut*. You like Kubrick, right?

SLOAT: *Love* Kubrick. My favorite.

DEVYN: So you know *Eyes Wide Shut*. Well, from a certain angle, you can see the couple's marriage as a metaphor for the relationship between Kubrick and us, a romance between artist and audience.

SLOAT: Oh, that's really interesting. So are we Tom Cruise, and is Kubrick Nicole Kidman? We're driven by a kind of jealousy of other fans—that kind of thing?

DEVYN: Hm, I think that works, too. But I was thinking of it the other way around. For me, Cruise is Kubrick, worrying about Kidman—his true audience—being unfaithful with other filmmakers. Kidman is us—the true audience. We're tempted by attractive alternatives, by other directors, but we resist the temptation. We don't give in.

SLOAT: That's really interesting. You've got some mind, Ms. Gail.

*She snuggles in.*

DEVYN: Thanks for noticing.

INT. MARTIAL ARTS DOJO – NIGHT

*A martial arts training hall with wall-to-wall puzzle mats, striking targets, etc. At the front is no national flag but a vertical ban-*

ner with the Japanese character "jitsu" (術) above the character "do" (道), a large yin-yang symbol, and in the middle a small black-and-white photograph, framed, a portrait of a kneeling subject, presumably the art's founder. Opposite the front wall, near the entrance, is a corner desk beside an open locker room door. Various STUDENTS in white gis and belts of various ranks stand around talking, some stretching. They are barefoot. The belts should follow the ITF taekwondo hierarchy. DAN, wearing a black belt with two stripes, is among them, as is another BLACK BELT without stripes, and a YELLOW BELT. Behind the desk stands MA'AM, also barefoot and in a gi, with five stripes on her black belt. Her hair falls in alternating streaks of dark and blonde. Off to the side, in regular athletic wear, also barefoot, are SLOAT and another NEWCOMER. The gi-clad students are notably relaxed, while Sloat and the other newcomer nod at each other uncertainly. After a moment, Ma'am shouts...

MA'AM: *Line up!*

*The students line up in descending order of rank, from the front of the room, right to left, in rows of three. Dan stands top right, the other Black Belt to his left, etc. They stand with legs shoulder-width apart and arms straight down before them with hands fisted. After the other students line up, Sloat and the other newcomer tentatively approach, then line up to the left of the yellow belt, who gestures to them where to stand.*

MA'AM (*to Dan*): Sir, will you do joints, please?

DAN (*bowing*): Yes, Ma'am.

*Dan moves to the front and stands at attention, feet together and arms at his sides. Everyone else stands likewise. He turns to bow to the back wall as the class bows with him. He turns again to the class.*

DAN (CONT'D): To the front.

*He bows to the class as the class bows back. He then leads the class through a series of joint warmup stretches with 10–12 cycles of each before moving to the next instruction.*

DAN (CONT'D): Neck forward and back... Left and right... Ear to shoulder... Shoulders forward... Backward... Crisscrossing arms... Hip rotations... Other direction... Knee bends... Calf raises... And ankles... Other ankle....

*He stops, standing at attention, looking at Ma'am. She strides to* the front, exchanges bows with Dan, taking his place at the front as he returns to his place in line. She exchanges bows with the class.

MA'AM: We'll start with one-two-switches, my pace. *Fighting stance!*

*Everyone adopts a bladed orthodox fighting stance, hands up, although Sloat and the other newcomer are slow to get there. The class mirrors Ma'am as she throws a jab-cross combo, then does a jump stance switch, then repeats in a southpaw stance, switching back to orthodox, and so on. With each strike, Ma'am and the students KIHAP (shout "Hi!"), the students at a lower volume.*

MA'AM: Come on! Let me hear you breathe.

*The students kihap louder. Ma'am nods, continuing the cycle. The class falls into a cohesive rhythm. Sloat's eyes are intent, task-focused. He has found the rhythm and begins to smile. Later. Sloat and the other newcomer, hectic and sweaty, are off to the side. Sloat finishes toweling off, then inverts a water bottle, taking a long drink. The other newcomer seems rushed in preparing to leave. He avoids eye contact. Ma'am approaches. The other newcomer beats a hasty retreat. Ma'am watches him leave.*

MA'AM: So, what do you think?

SLOAT (*beaming*): That was great, Ma'am. A lot of fun. Sign me up.

MA'AM: Good. You can sign up now or do the paperwork online.

*He smiles.*

SLOAT: Will do.

INT. ROMI'S HOUSE – TV ROOM – NIGHT (LATER)

*ROMI is reclined on the couch, her feet up. She holds an open book, a floor lamp behind her throwing light on the pages and, in the view from the foyer, backlighting her. She is reading, very much at leisure. We hear the SOUNDS of the front door being unlocked and pushed open. SLOAT enters, dishevelled, sweaty, still beaming. He locks the door behind him and puts down his backpack.*

SLOAT: Hey.

*Her eyes lift from the page to scrutinize him.*

ROMI: It's late. What took you?

SLOAT: Remember? I tried that jitsu do class.

ROMI: Yes, you did say that.

SLOAT: Oh, it was great. It feels like I learned a lot from just one class. And so much fun.

ROMI: So you'll be going back?

SLOAT: Paid a month in advance already.
ROMI: Do you think that's wise? You're up for renewal. You should really concentrate on that, if you have any hope of getting tenure.
SLOAT: I've got irons in the fire. You know that.
ROMI: But what irons? What fires? You should be more selective.
SLOAT: Besides, in a way I think this will help, with focus, balance, life in general.
ROMI: We'll see.

> *His enthusiasm ebbs. He looks at her steadily. She goes back to her reading.*

SLOAT: Look, listen, there's something I need to tell you.
ROMI: Not now.
SLOAT: It's important. We really should talk.
ROMI: Do you not know what "Not now" means? *God.*
SLOAT: Okay.

> *He looks away, puzzled, picks up his backpack, standing still for a moment.*

INT. UNIVERSITY LIBRARY – DEVYN'S OFFICE – DAY

> *An office off the stacks on one of the upper floors of the library, smaller but newer-looking than Sloat's. A window looks out on a small section of roof continuous with the floor, a large window that opens. A desk with laptop, books, and assorted papers faces a single chair for visitors. DEVYN sits at the desk, alternately looking something up on the laptop and typing something in. We hear KNOCKING followed by...*

SLOAT (O.S.): Too busy for a visit?

> *She looks up, smiling.*

DEVYN: Not at all. Just finishing up some acquisitions. I'm glad you came.
SLOAT: Had some time before class. Thought I'd drop in.

> *He pulls out a chair.*

DEVYN: Wait.

> *She rummages in a desk drawer. She holds up a pack of cigarettes and disposable lighter, an impish look on her face.*

DEVYN (CONT'D): Let's step out of my office.
SLOAT: Ooh, you're bad.
DEVYN: Uh-uh. Guess again, although I'm not exactly a classic good girl, am I?

SLOAT: Works for me.
DEVYN: I *know*. Come on.
> She cranks open the window, steps through, then reaches back for his hand.

EXT. UNIVERSITY COLLEGE – ROOF – CONTINUOUS
> The roof section is small and square, with only a short, inadequate border at the edge, maybe a foot high. It is several stories above the building's main entrance. It is an overcast day but otherwise pleasant and mild. DEVYN reaches back through the open window to help SLOAT step through to the roof. They take in the view.

DEVYN: Some view, huh? Come on.
> She springs over to the edge, while he reaches out as if to warn or stop her. She turns, smiles, and beckons him over.

DEVYN: Come on.
> He approaches cautiously, mindful of the danger to both of them. The pavement seems a long way down.

SLOAT (O.S.): Jesus.
> We hear the SCUFF of him pulling back. The color has drained from his face and flushed hers.

SLOAT (CONT'D): That's a vertiginous height.
DEVYN: Isn't it?
> They step back, away from the edge.

DEVYN: You okay?
SLOAT: I'm okay. I'm okay.
> She lights a cigarette, offers him the pack, which he waves off.

DEVYN: You sure? It'll calm your nerves.
SLOAT: I'm sure.
> He takes a breath, recovered now.

SLOAT (CONT'D): I wanted to give you an update on the Thol investigation.
DEVYN: You sound like a detective out of film noir. You forgot your trench coat. (*Doing Bogart*) Shay, gimme the lowdown on this Thol character.
SLOAT: I can't find anything on Minerva's Perch, the publisher. It doesn't seem to be a registered business. It's kind of a dead end, except I think Minerva's Perch is just Thol himself.
DEVYN: The books are self-published?
SLOAT: That's what I'm thinking. These novels are *un*conventional,

to say the least. It would hardly surprise me if Thol had to—or chose to—put them out himself.
>She takes a drag, EXHALES.

DEVYN: Does that lessen the work in your eyes?

SLOAT: Not at all. Not really, although in some ways it makes my job harder—in some ways.

DEVYN: If you're right that "Jonas Thol" is a pseudonym, I guess we have a wedge between self-publishing and vanity press.

SLOAT: Good point.

DEVYN: So where does all that leave you?

SLOAT: If Minerva's Perch just is Jonas Thol, then the printer likely had direct dealings with Thol himself—Leisure Works Printing, right down the road.

DEVYN: That *is* a lead. But you're getting all twisted up over this. Ease off a bit.
>She hugs him.

DEVYN (CONT'D): I don't want you obsessing about anyone but me. Anyway, shouldn't the work speak for itself—all that "death of the author" stuff? Especially if that's the way Thol wants it.
>Beat. He blinks, looking up at the sky.

SLOAT: Was that rain?
>She looks at him.

INT. UNIVERSITY COLLEGE – CLASSROOM – DAY

>A small university classroom with a capacity of several dozen people, windows at the back spilling natural light over rows of tables and chairs divided into two sections with an aisle in the middle. At the front are a lectern, and a blackboard and whiteboard with a screen partially blocking both. Around fifteen STUDENTS are scattered throughout, either in twosomes or alone. Their clothing and bearing suggest a degree of maturity belonging to juniors or seniors. Among them are SYDNEY, a redhead, near the front, STUDENT 1 and STUDENT 2 sitting together on the aisle, and STUDENT 3 sitting alone in the back. SLOAT enters with backpack and travel mug, putting both on the lectern. He gives a brief, closed-lips smile, then opens the backpack and removes his laptop and a folder of notes, which he opens, touching the first page. Then he checks his watch, returns to close the still-open door, and returns to the lectern. He hunts for something on the lectern, then looks at

*the blackboard, walking over to pick up chalk and write "MDS 315" on the board before turning back to the lectern and surveying the audience.*

SLOAT: Welcome to MDS 315: Applied Topics in Meta-Disciplinary Studies. This is my first time doing an elective here at Arcana, so I look forward to it. Some of you might have had me for intro two years ago, though I'm not recognizing any faces…

*He notices Sydney.*

SLOAT (CONT'D):… except you. Sydney with a "Y," right? Like in *D.O.A.* Did I make that connection before?

*She nods.*

SLOAT (CONT'D): So, thanks to you all for signing up. I hope that the course doesn't disappoint. I've designed a series of texts and other cultural items for a sustained meta-disciplinary analysis over the term—to give an emergent sense of the state of the art in M-DS. No heavy lifting today, however. I want to go over the syllabus, have a look at the class schedule. All readings are available online, as usual. One thing I should note is that in this course, I don't expect you to just know the material from an M-DS perspective. I'm hoping that as we explore applications of M-DS, you'll actually be *doing* M-DS yourselves, adding something to the discourse.

*He pauses to take a sip of coffee, survey the room again, and give another closed-lips smile.*

SLOAT (CONT'D): Okay, let's get to it.

*The students open notebooks and laptops, priming pens and fingers.*

INT. SLOAT'S CAR – DAY

*SLOAT is driving with DEVYN in the passenger seat. They are on a paved country road, the same road leading from the highway exit to Foxbridge Cross but outbound on the other side of town.*

SLOAT: I'm glad you decided to come with me.
DEVYN: My pleasure. I want to support you, to be with you for this. Oh, I forgot.

*She pulls out her phone, starts texting.*

SLOAT: What is it?
DEVYN: Nothing, nothing important. A work thing I should have taken care of.

*She finishes texting and puts the phone away. We hear the TONE of a response, which Devyn ignores.*

DEVYN: Where is this place, anyway?
SLOAT: On the right. Coming up soon.
>They come to a stretch of road blending an industrial park with strip malls. They pull into a strip mall parking lot on the right and park facing a storefront with a sign that reads "Leisure Works Printing". He turns off the engine.

INT. "LEISURE WORKS PRINTING" – CONTINUOUS
>*A print shop that also does bookbinding. A counter across the front separates the customer area from the front work area, with desks and photocopiers. A doorway leads to the back room from which we hear the chunky repetitive SOUNDS of a print run. The PRINTER, a gruff-looking, burly man in flannel shirt and jeans, stands at the counter, working on a computer. SLOAT, holding his backpack, and DEVYN enter, summoning the CHIME of a bell. Devyn falls in behind Sloat. The printer looks up, holds her in his gaze for a moment, then shifts to him.*

PRINTER: How can I help you?
SLOAT: Hi, I'm Dr. John Sloat, from the university.
>*Sloat smiles, takes out his wallet and flips it open. He holds it up for the printer. In the ID window we see Sloat's faculty card. The printer restrains an amused smile.*

PRINTER: Okay, Dr. Sloat. Well?
SLOAT: I left a couple messages, but I never heard back.
PRINTER: Oh, yes, Sloat. Sorry about that. It's our busy season.
SLOAT: Understandable. I'm hoping you can help me with a mystery, a literary mystery.
>*He takes three books out of his backpack and lines them up on the counter. It is Thol's trilogy: the gray WHERE WISE MEN NEVER GO, the black THE NEXT THING, and the white UP AGAINST BEYOND.*

SLOAT (CONT'D): You printed these, yes?
PRINTER: That's right.
SLOAT: Did you have any direct dealing with the author, Jonas Thol?
PRINTER: I don't know any Jonas Thol.
SLOAT: That's a pen name, probably. Who's your contact at Minerva's Perch?
PRINTER: I don't see how my business is any business of yours.
SLOAT: But you don't understand, this is *great* work. It's important— but it's gone under the radar. Hardly anybody knows it even exists. The

author deserves to be known—to be… celebrated.
PRINTER: Maybe so, but even if I did know, I wouldn't tell you. I'd respect their wishes. What matters is their privacy, not your curiosity.
*The printer shakes his head.*
PRINTER (CONT'D): Academics, all alike. I have work to do.
SLOAT: If I could just explain…
*The printer leans on the counter, his arms flexed.*
PRINTER: I have work to do.

INT. SLOAT'S CAR – LATER
*The car faces Leisure Works Printing as before. SLOAT and DEVYN get in, closing the doors.*
SLOAT: Jesus. What's his problem?
DEVYN: I don't know.
SLOAT: All I wanted was some information—about a customer. It's not like there's any client confidentiality here. He's not a doctor or lawyer.
DEVYN: I know. But he has a point. It's not as though you have a right to know who his clients are. You're not a police detective conducting some criminal investigation.
SLOAT: No, you're right. But this was a solid lead. It could have broken the case.
DEVYN: Anyway, you're not going to get any answers from him.
SLOAT: But it's got to be in his records. If I could get in there—or hire someone, maybe a private eye.
DEVYN: The files are password-protected, most likely. Finding out isn't so easy in real life, even for a pro.
*She puts a hand on his arm.*
DEVYN (CONT'D): I'm worried, John. I'm worried that you're thinking about this all wrong, that you're missing what really matters.
*He puts his hand on hers, holds her gaze, then lets go of both. Then he turns the ignition, which we hear GRIND at first, then RUMBLE smooth.*

INT. ROMI'S HOUSE – TV ROOM – NIGHT
*ROMI is sitting on the couch, turned to face the foyer, her legs crossed, her top foot oscillating. She is not quite her usual calm. She SNIFFS, tightens her lips, then looks away from the foyer. We hear the SOUNDS of the door being unlocked and pushed open.*

*SLOAT enters, closing and locking the door behind him. He kicks off his shoes, takes off his jacket and hangs it up, speaking before looking.*

SLOAT: Hey. A definite chill in the air. You okay?

ROMI: Where have you been? It's late.

SLOAT: Remember? Poker night. Guess what? I broke even.

ROMI: You're lying.

SLOAT: No. I did get lucky a few times—on a few hands.

ROMI: Are you having an affair?

*They lock eyes.*

SLOAT: Yes.

ROMI: Who is it?

SLOAT: Does it matter? Someone at Arcana… Devyn Gail.

ROMI: Devyn Gail? The *librarian*? That mousy little *nothing*? What the fuck, John. You prefer *that* to *this*?

SLOAT: I'm sorry. I should have told you. I tried, but…

ROMI: You really are that dumb, aren't you? You think I'm just going to roll over and take this? Not on your worthless, miserable little life. Are you leaving me?

SLOAT: Yes.

ROMI: You think so? You've got another thing coming, *ass*hole!

*She steadies herself, then smiles.*

ROMI (CONT'D): It's not going to be that easy. You're up for renewal. You meet with the Tenure and Promotions Committee—what?—next week? Imagine what the right *wrong* word from me would do to you. You'd be finished. You know how lucky you are even to have this job? You think another position like this is just going to fall into your lap? No, you're not going to leave me for… *that*. You're going to end it—now.

SLOAT: I'll move my things out.

ROMI: We'll see about that.

INT. UNIVERSITY COLLEGE – CHAIR'S OFFICE – DAY

*SLOAT is sitting in a visitor's chair, facing the CHAIR sitting at her desk.*

SLOAT: Some game the other night.

CHAIR: Yeah. Can't win 'em all. But you came out ahead, didn't you?

SLOAT: Broke even. Lost that big hand at the end.

CHAIR: Right. On to business then.

SLOAT: If we must.
CHAIR: We must. Wise of you to give me a draft of your application before submitting. There's still time to make changes before you meet with Tenure and Promotions.
SLOAT: Okay.
CHAIR: Your teaching and service are fine—for junior faculty. I'd like to see your numbers a bit higher, but no cause for concern.
SLOAT: Good.
CHAIR: As for the research agenda: well-written, well-argued. But you've forgotten what I said about consensus significance—still pursuing a line on a writer nobody cares about.
SLOAT: Author, yes. But did you note that my article on Thol is forthcoming in *J. M-DS*? With respect, I'm not ignoring your advice. I'm trying to overcome the obstacle, and to establish what may become, *should* become, consensus significance on Thol's work. It's *that* good. It's amazing. It could change lives.
CHAIR: Oh, hardly. Heed your own words here. Even if you've got a toehold on consensus significance, that doesn't mean you have a leg to stand on. You're not recognized in the literature. The T&P Committee simply will not see this in a favorable light—even a light you're trying to shed, or that deserves to be shed.
SLOAT: What do you suggest?
CHAIR: You need to decide if you're on board, *really* on board, or not. Think hard. There's still time.

INT. MARTIAL ARTS DOJO – NIGHT

> *The STUDENTS are lined up and standing at attention, with DAN at the head of the class and his line space empty top right next to BLACK BELT. At the back, to the left of the YELLOW BELT, stands SLOAT in a uniform with a white belt. MA'AM strides to the head of the class and exchanges bows with Dan. Dan returns to his place in line. Ma'am exchanges bows with the entire class.*

MA'AM: We have a test coming up soon. The date and time are TBD. Your forms I'm happy with, so tonight is all about drilling belt-level skills. I'll be assessing you to determine whether you're ready—if you've put in the work, which many of you have. If you're ready, you'll get a ticket at the end of class. We have an even number, so everybody pair up.

*The students pair off with one another, each pair at a similar belt level. Sloat and the yellow belt nod at each other and move a little closer together.*

MA'AM: We'll begin with striking. Get to it.

*The pairs spread out on the mat, finding their own space. Later. Sloat and the yellow belt are drilling kick combinations. The yellow belt is holding a shield for Sloat. The other pairs are drilling more difficult kick combinations. Sloat takes an orthodox fighting stance, while the yellow belt holds the shield over his torso, standing in open stance opposite. Sloat throws a rear-leg roundhouse into the pad, switching to southpaw. The yellow belt steps back and holds the shield in front as Sloat transitions to a stepping side kick. Ma'am walks slowly into view and stops, watching. The yellow belt and Sloat reset, starting with southpaw, and perform the same combination on the other side: rear-leg roundhouse into orthodox stepping side kick. Ma'am walks on to the next pair. Later. The yellow belt and Sloat are drilling basic hip throws using a crash mat. The other pairs are doing more jiu jitsu–style transitions on the regular mat. Sloat attacks the yellow belt with a half-speed right punch. The yellow belt grabs Sloat's forearm and does a smooth right hip throw, spinning Sloat onto the crash mat. Ma'am walks slowly into view and stops, watching. The yellow belt and Sloat switch places. The yellow belt comes at Sloat in the same way, with a half-speed right punch. Sloat does a right hip throw, but it is rougher, more forced than the yellow belt's.*

MA'AM: Hang on. Be decisive. Commit to it. When you see that punch coming, that's your cue to step. Don't forget to turn your right foot inward 45 degrees. If the timing's right, you'll present the hip for the final turn, and he'll just flip right over, like that (*snaps fingers*). Slow it down in your mind. Again.

*They reset. The yellow belt's right fist comes at Sloat, turning over in a right cross. Sloat's eyes narrow. His right foot steps forward, turning inward 45 degrees. Sloat's hip throw is much better this time, skillful and seemingly effortless. He looks at Ma'am, whose only reaction is to walk on. He smiles to himself, giving a slight nod. Later. The students are filing by the desk on their way out, some in their uniforms but most in street clothes. Ma'am hands small paper tickets to some, not others. Sloat, in street clothes, with a gear bag slung over his shoulder, approaches the desk behind a pair of students. Ma'am gives a ticket to one but not the other, then looks down at the desk. Sloat takes another step and stops. Ma'am looks up at him.*

INT. UNIVERSITY COLLEGE – SLOAT'S OFFICE – DAY
*SLOAT is sitting at his desk, a stack of essays neglected beside his open laptop. He stares at the screen. The screen shows a word-processing file, which reads...*

JOHN SLOAT—RESEARCH OUTLINE

AS AN ASSISTANT PROFESSOR IN META-DISCIPLINARY STUDIES, I PLAN TO FOCUS MY RESEARCH ON VARIOUS TOPICS BASED ON AN ANALYSIS OF THE WORKS OF JONAS THOL.

ALTHOUGH THOL'S WORK IS NOT WIDELY KNOWN, I HAVE BEGUN TO ESTABLISH ITS CONSENSUS SIGNIFICANCE IN A FORTHCOMING ARTICLE DERIVED FROM A CONFERENCE PRESENTATION AT THE INTERNATIONAL ASSOCIATION OF META-DISCIPLINARY STUDIES:

SLOAT, J. (IN PRESS): "JONAS THOL: A NEW DIRECTION IN WRITING", JOURNAL OF META-DISCIPLINARY STUDIES.

*The cursor drags to select the first two paragraphs. Sloat SIGHS. A CLICK deletes the paragraphs. The cursor winks above the bibliographic reference. We hear KNOCKING at the door. Another CLICK undoes the deletion. Sloat closes the laptop.*
SLOAT: One sec!
*He gets up, goes to open the door. DEVYN is standing in the doorway. She smiles coyly.*
DEVYN: Want to grab a coffee? My treat. Is it too late for caf?
*She enters, then closes the door discretely. She turns back to Sloat, sliding her arms around him.*
DEVYN: Something I want to tell you.
*He tightens his lips. He removes her hands, gently but firmly.*
DEVYN: Uh-oh. Should I open the door, Professor?
SLOAT: Maybe.
DEVYN: Uh-oh.

SLOAT: Maybe you should sit.
DEVYN: Maybe I should stand.
>*He tightens his lips again, then looks away. She studies his face.*

DEVYN (CONT'D): So that's it?—after everything. After everything we've been. After everything we are to each other.
SLOAT: I'm afraid so.
>*She puts on a brave face.*

DEVYN: Don't be afraid.
>*She collapses into him, throwing her arms around his neck.*

DEVYN (CONT'D): No, no, no, no.
>*He puts his arms around her.*

SLOAT: It's not so bad.
>*She looks up at him through tears, her smile anguished.*

DEVYN: No, it's not so bad—it's worse.
>*We see them from a distance.*

INT. UNIVERSITY COLLEGE – SLOAT'S OFFICE – NIGHT
>*SLOAT is sitting at his desk, marking essays with a red pen. He is about halfway through the stack. Also on his desk are his laptop, closed, cell phone, face down, and travel mug. He reads quickly, now and then circling or crossing out something on the page, adding a brief note. He flips to the next page, the last. Beat. He makes another correction, scrawls a large "B+", then adds an indecipherable summary comment. He tosses the essay face down on the marked stack. He takes a sip from the travel mug. We hear the TONE of a text notification. He SIGHS, picking up the phone. We see a series of unanswered text messages from "Devyn," reading…*

- *HEY*
- *ARE YOU THERE?*
- *I DON'T LIKE THE WAY WE LEFT THINGS*
- *CAN WE MEET?*
- *JUST FOR COFFEE*
- *CAN WE TALK AT LEAST?*
- *I NEED TO SEE YOU*
- *WHY WON'T YOU ANSWER?*
- *PLEASE ANSWER*
- *PLEASE*
- *PLEASE!!!!!*

> *The ellipsis of a forthcoming text appears. He taps the "Devyn" icon, then "info", then scrolls down to select "Block This Caller". He puts the phone face-down on the desk. He opens his laptop, logs in, and clicks into his email. There are a dozen new messages in a row, all from "Devyn Gail" with blank subject lines. He deletes them quickly, one by one, without opening any. He empties his email trash. His office phone RINGS once, twice. The caller ID shows, "Private Number". He picks up on the third ring.*

SLOAT: This is John Sloat... No, look, listen... No... No... That's not true... No... That's not what I said.

> *A long pause during which his face is attentive but calm, not quite impassive. Then his calm begins to break.*

SLOAT (CONT'D): Oh, don't say that... Don't do that... Don't do anything... Wait. Just wait. I'll be right there, okay? Okay?

> *He hangs up, EXHALES sharply, then rushes out, leaving the office door open.*

INT. UNIVERSITY COLLEGE – HALLWAYS – CONTINUOUS

> *SLOAT is moving down the hallway. His feet move first in a hasty walk, then a purposeful jog, then finally a run. We follow him through several turns and hallways, seeing no one until he approaches the library. Two STUDENTS ahead of Sloat approach the library together. One peels off and reverses course while the other carries on and enters. Sloat slows his pace to a brisk walk.*

INT. UNIVERSITY COLLEGE – LIBRARY – CONTINUOUS

> *There are STUDENTS studying at tables, others in line at the circulation desk with some STAFF on duty. SLOAT enters and crosses to a stairwell, pushing through the heavy door. He takes the stairs two at a time. His BREATHING becomes heavy. He grabs handrails to help propel him up the remaining flights of stairs. He pushes through another stairwell door, slowing to a walk with stacks on one side and doors on the other. He approaches an office door, standing open, with "Devyn Gail" on the nameplate.*

SLOAT: Devyn?

> *He cautiously peeks into the office.*

INT. UNIVERSITY COLLEGE – DEVYN'S OFFICE – CONTIN-

UOUS
> *SLOAT enters.*

SLOAT: Devyn?
> *The office is empty. The window to the roof is wide open. He crosses to it and looks out. DEVYN is standing at the edge of the roof with her back to him.*

EXT. UNIVERSITY COLLEGE – ROOF – CONTINUOUS
> *SLOAT steps one foot through the window, keeping his eyes on DEVYN as much as possible.*

SLOAT: Hey.
> *No answer. He pulls the other foot through.*

SLOAT (CONT'D): You okay?
> *She shakes her head, still facing away from him.*

SLOAT (CONT'D): I'm here.
> *She turns around, forces a smile.*

SLOAT: It's okay.
> *She takes a step and starts to circle—slowly—toward him as they talk, and with each step she takes he circles away, keeping the same distance between them.*

DEVYN: I still mean something to you.

SLOAT: Of course you do.

DEVYN: What do you think of the idea—just the idea—if it ever feels right, only if it feels right, of giving it another chance?
> *They have now switched places, with Devyn at the window, Sloat at the edge of the roof.*

DEVYN (CONT'D): It could be… everything.
> *She takes a step forward. His heel SCUFFS into the low barrier, which momentarily upsets his balance.*

DEVYN (CONT'D): Don't we deserve another chance? What we have, what we are—it's so much. It means so much.

SLOAT: I wish I could give you that.

DEVYN: But you can. All it would take is a word, a single word.
> *She opens her arms, looks around.*

DEVYN (CONT'D): This is life, John, and life is a question—one you can't avoid. So what's your answer going to be? Everything can be wonderful again if you just say that one little word. Say yes, John. Just say yes.

EXT. ARCANA UNIVERSITY – UNIVERSITY COLLEGE – DAY

*SLOAT walks toward the entrance on the paved walkway. He sips from his travel mug, shrugs under his backpack. As he approaches the door, something to the right on the pavement draws his attention. It is a police outline of a body with bloodstains at the head. It is the same outline in the opening scene. We now see that it lies perpendicular to the side of the building. Sloat steps forward, looking down, his face neutral with a faint suggestion of curiosity. He blinks. Beat.*

JENSON (O.S.): What the absolute fuck.

*JENSON steps forward, stopping beside Sloat. Sloat, still looking down, takes a sip of coffee.*

JENSON (CONT'D): A little early in the semester for student suicides, isn't it? Wonder if one of our esteemed colleagues finally saw the light.

*Sloat looks at him.*

INT. UNIVERSITY COLLEGE – DEPARTMENT MAILROOM – DAY

*SLOAT stands at his mail slot, his travel mug beside him on the counter. He taps the bottom of his empty mail slot with his fingers, then reaches for his travel mug, stops before touching it. He glances at a single package beside him. It is oddly but dully yellow. He angles his neck to read. His eyes widen, then narrow. It is addressed to "Dr. John Sloat, Meta-disciplinary Studies, Arcana University", sent by "Devyn Gail, University College Library, Arcana University". He frowns at the box, turns as if to leave. Then he stops and turns back, tucks the travel mug under his arm, picks up the package, and leaves.*

INT. UNIVERSITY COLLEGE – SLOAT'S OFFICE – DAY (LATER)

*The yellow box rests in an empty chair. SLOAT is sitting at his desk with his laptop open. He clicks on the email icon. Among a dozen or so unremarkable new messages is one from "Office of the President", with subject line "Recent Tragedy on Campus". Sloat moves the cursor to the email, waits for a moment, then clicks on it. We read...*

> To All Members of the Arcana University Community:
>
> It is with profound sadness that we announce the death of a well-known and respected member of the Arcana family, Devyn Gail...

*Sloat looks relatively impassive, but his inner eyebrows lower with a shade more intensity. The email continues...*

> ... Last night, Campus Security responded to a call at University College, where the body was found.
>
> Police are investigating the incident and have asked that anyone with information concerning the incident come forward immediately. Further details will be provided when available.

*Sloat's eyes edge wider. He sits back in his chair and looks off into the distance.*

### INT. UNIVERSITY COLLEGE – SLOAT'S OFFICE – DAY

*The yellow package remains untouched on the chair in the corner. SLOAT stands at the window, meditatively looking out. His laptop is open on the desk. The TONE of a new email notification shakes him alert. He goes to his desk, sits down, and clicks on the only unread message at the top, from "AllAboutThol" with the subject line "3 Clues" and timestamped "3:15 pm". He clicks on the email. We read...*

> I want you to know what you want to know.
> Expect three clues at the appointed time.

*He frowns at the screen, and puts his hand to his chin, sitting back in his chair.*

### INT. UNIVERSITY COLLEGE – SLOAT'S OFFICE – DAY

*The yellow package remains undisturbed on the chair in the corner. We hear the SOUND of a key unlocking the door. SLOAT enters,* backpack on, carrying his travel mug and a stack of papers. He puts down the travel mug, drops the stack to SLAP on the desktop, then removes his laptop from the backpack, opening it on the desk. He leans toward the screen, then logs in, still standing. He stretches his arms overhead, GROANING before sitting down. He clicks on the email icon. Among a handful of new messages is one from "AllAboutThol" with the subject line "Clue #1" and timestamped "3:15 pm". He clicks on the email, which reads…

>    TAKE NOTE, IN HUNTING WHAT YOU SEEK,
>    OF THOL YOU'VE HAD MORE THAN A PEEK.

SLOAT: "Take note, in hunting what you seek… of Thol you've had more than a peek".

INT. UNIVERSITY COLLEGE – SLOAT'S OFFICE – DAY

*SLOAT is sitting at his desk in the same position, typing on his laptop. He is wearing a different shirt. The yellow package remains undisturbed on the chair in the corner. The stack of papers is gone. The clock on the wall shows 3:15. He stops typing to glance at the clock, then does a slow set of alternating ear-to-shoulder neck stretches. He takes a deep breath, looks again at the clock, then resumes typing, fast and rhythmic. We hear the TONE of a new email notification. He stops typing and clicks on the open email tab. We see one new message. It is from "AllAboutThol" with the subject line "Clue #2" and timestamped "3:15 pm". He clicks on the email, which reads…*

>    AN AUTHOR'S NAME IS BODIES TWO,
>    BOTH WHICH ALREADY KNOWN BY YOU.

SLOAT: "An author's name is bodies two, both which already known by you".

INT. UNIVERSITY COLLEGE – CAFÉ – DAY

*SLOAT and JENSON are at the counter. An aproned CASHIER stands waiting. Sloat pays for their coffee. They turn and walk over to the self-serve station.*

SLOAT: I'm telling you, they know. They know who Thol really is.

*Sloat takes two paper cups from the stack and hands one over. Jenson starts filling his cup.*

JENSON: Maybe. Maybe they're just jerking you around, trying to wind you up. Something I might do.

*Jenson finishes filling his cup, puts on a plastic cap. While Sloat fills his cup, puts in milk, and puts on a cap, we hear...*

SLOAT: No, something in the tone, I don't know. An intuition. Not intuitive, but there's something there. "Of Thol you've had more than a peek"—they know that *I* know the work, well, thoroughly. And "bodies two, both which already known by you". That has to mean the body of work and—what?—the man himself?

*Sloat takes a sip. Jenson takes a sip.*

JENSON: Maybe. Maybe the other body, if there is another body, is—I don't know, a body of lies, or some mindless object, a corpse, all that "death of the author" stuff.

SLOAT: Which would make me right, after all.

JENSON: Anyway, why are you still hung up on this? Remember what the Chair said. There's absolutely no consensus significance to this, none at all. Even if you're right, it's the wrong move. You should be worried about tenure, not some pet distraction. You're up for renewal *this year*. Get tenure first, then you can pursue any passion project you want. Don't leave me here all bleak and friendless. Hard enough here without all that bullshit.

INT. UNIVERSITY COLLEGE – CLASSROOM – DAY

*SLOAT stands at the lectern, teaching. There are about eight students present, including SYDNEY, STUDENT 1, STUDENT 2, and STUDENT 3. The screen behind Sloat is blank. Sloat looks at his watch.*

SLOAT: We've got some time left, so I'd like to shift gears to something a little different. I've mentioned more than once—haven't I?—my favorite writer, Jonas Thol.

*Sydney and a few others nod.*

SLOAT (CONT'D): Well, I haven't had you read any of his work, because as brilliant as it is, it's too peripheral, for now at least. I'm hoping to change that. Part of my research aims to uncover the person behind (*air-quoting*) "Jonas Thol", which seems to be a *nom de plume*. Now, I haven't had any luck finding out who Thol is. But I've received three mysterious emails purporting to reveal—in riddle form—Thol's secret

identity. I'm hoping we can work through these clues together, and maybe solve the mystery. Are you game?
> *Sydney nods eagerly, a few others half-heartedly.*

SLOAT (CONT'D): Okay, then. Here are the clues.
> *He clicks a slide onto the screen, which reads...*

### WHO IS JONAS THOL?

<u>Clues</u>

(1) *Take note, in hunting what you seek, of Thol you've had more than a peek.*

(2) *An author's name is bodies two, both which already known by you.*

(3) *Like Thol, you work in span of fox, but think too much outside the box.*

SLOAT (CONT'D): Consider each on your own before we continue.
> *Sloat turns to look at the screen, and gives the students time to read, maybe fifteen seconds, before he continues. Sydney, Student 1, Student 2, and Student 3 are attentive, the other students less engaged.*

SLOAT (CONT'D): Here's my thinking. In Clue #1, "of Thol you've had more than a peek": that suggests I know what Thol looks like, that I've seen him in the flesh.
> *A few nods.*

SLOAT (CONT'D): This seems confirmed in Clue #2: "bodies two, both which already known to you"—body of work, that's one, presumably, and the physical person, that's two.

SYDNEY: But "known *by* you", doesn't that imply something else? Maybe the preposition matters. I mean, if you know Thol—without knowing you know—it could be... well, anyone you know. It could be any one of us.

SLOAT: Sydney, are you Jonas Thol?
> *She cocks an eyebrow. He holds her gaze, then breaks off.*

SLOAT (CONT'D): As for Clue #3, I assume "span of fox" is just a pun on "Foxbridge". So, Thol's a local. But what about "too much outside the box"?

STUDENT 3: Well, "inside the box" clearly means conventional. So thinking "too much outside the box" must mean too unconventional.

SLOAT: That does make sense, although thinking outside the box is supposed to be a good thing. And Thol's work is so unconventional. Clue #3 just doesn't fit.

STUDENT 1: Or maybe it's not idiomatic. Maybe the riddler means your thinking is too abstract, or something—that you should refocus on more earthy, grounded things, you know, *inside* the box.

*Student 2 slaps Student 1's arm in playful reproach.*

SLOAT: All interesting takes. Anything else?

*Beat.*

SYDNEY: What if the box isn't a metaphor, but something physical, something box-like, like a building?

*Sloat nods. Beat. He looks at his watch.*

SLOAT: Thanks for indulging me in this. Your comments have been helpful. That's it for today.

*The students gather their belongings and begin to file out. Sloat closes his laptop and starts packing up. The room now otherwise empty, Sydney approaches the lectern, stopping at a respectful distance.*

SYDNEY: Do you have a minute?

SLOAT: Sure.

INT. UNIVESRITY COLLEGE – SLOAT'S OFFICE – DAY

*Sloat's laptop is open on his desk and shows the slide with three riddles. The yellow package remains undisturbed on the chair in the corner. SLOAT is agitated, pacing back and forth at his desk in fits and starts, now and then rubbing his face with his hands. He is MUTTERING to himself indistinctly, repeating the same inarticulate phrase and bobbing his head side-to-side to the rhythm. The sound becomes intelligible.*

SLOAT: "You think too much outside the box". You think too much outside the box.

*He wheels around, slaps hands to lean on the desktop, staring at the screen.*

SLOAT (CONT'D): You think too much… outside the box… *outside* the box.

*He stares at the screen. He notices, beyond the screen in the corner chair, the yellow box. He sets down the yellow box firmly on the desk. He RUMMAGES in his desk. He uses scissors to slice through the packing tape across the top. He parts the cardboard to reveal*

> *a mostly full box. Above the packing material is an envelope with "For John" in Devyn's distinctive handwriting. He takes out the unsealed envelope, slides out a neatly folded letter. He leaves the envelope on the desk and walks over to the window, unfolding a letter in the same handwriting. He reads…*

DEVYN (V.O.): John, I couldn't bring myself to write "Dear John". The mere thought of it made me laugh, because of the irony. This isn't that kind of letter. As you know, I have shared your passion for Thol's writing for a long time, longer than you'd guess. So, it's time to tell you the answer you've been searching for. You deserve that…

> *His eyes widen as he reads on.*

DEVYN (V.O., CONT'D): Here, in this box, is all you'll need, not just to find the secret to Thol's true identity, but much more: all the material you'd need to spend a career on Thol, if you wanted to. You may be wondering why it took me so long to tell you, and why I'm telling you like this…

> *He nods before reading on.*

DEVYN (V.O., CONT'D): All I can say is, I'm not sure I can say. I suppose it's because I had such hopes for us. We really had something—something real and beautiful, but fragile, like so many beautiful things. I didn't want to change what we had, upset the delicate balance between us. I closed my eyes and hoped the dance would never end. If someone was going to break the rhythm, I didn't want it to be me. That's why I never told you, even though I wanted to, so much. I came close to telling you so many times. And so, my once true only, I leave you with this, with everything but a glimmer of hope for myself, and the strength perhaps to try again. All yours, always, Devyn

> *He lowers the letter slowly and looks out the window. Beat. He returns to the box, then pushes back the packing paper to reveal a manuscript titled "Untitled" by "Jonas Thol". He takes out the manuscript and angles it toward his face.*

SLOAT: I *knew* it. I knew there'd be a fourth book. I told you. But, how?

> *He flips through the manuscript hungrily, but then stops, EX-HALES to calm himself, and sets the manuscript down. He reaches back into the box, pulls out a reprint of his article, "Jonas Thol: A New Direction in Writing", which he quickly sets aside. Dipping into the box again, he pulls out a fair copy of the manuscript for WHERE WISE MEN NEVER GO. More measured this time, he*

*flips through the pages and sees various minor corrections in red ink—in Devyn's distinctive hand. He slaps the manuscript closed, looking askance.*

SLOAT: She was his *editor?*

*He puts down the fair copy manuscript and reaches once more—tentatively—into the box. He removes a large journal, which he opens to a random page. It is a handwritten text in Devyn's distinctive script.*

SLOAT (O.S.): Devyn…

*Beat. He flips back to the title page. We read the title "The First Gray Book" and the author "Devyn Gail"—both crossed out, with "Where Wise Men Never Go" and "Jonas Thol", respectively, written above with carets below. We stay here briefly. Sloat knits his brow. Back to the title page, where we linger a moment. Sloat's face cannot contain the shock of revelation. He stands completely still, palms open, as if he will never move again. The letter lies discarded on the floor, the whole display of evidence spread out on the desk before him.*

MONTAGE:

*Autumn scenes of the town and the Arcana University campus: colorful foliage, students in sweaters, etc. (In each of the following scenes, SLOAT is wearing a different outfit but the same blank expression.) He walks up the aisle, proctoring a test in his elective class classroom. The STUDENTS, including SYDNEY, STUDENT 1, STUDENT 2, and STUDENT 3, are spread out evenly, writing longhand in test booklets. He absently stirs milk into his travel mug coffee at the self-service station of the University College café. He stares past JENSON as Jenson talks inaudibly to him on the couch in the department mail room. He sits looking off in a department meeting lead by the CHAIR in a small seminar room, with ten FACULTY present, including JENSON. He unlocks his car, gets in, then pulls out of the University parking lot.*

INT. CHAIR'S HOUSE – BASEMENT – NIGHT

*Sitting at the poker table are THE CHAIR, JENSON, PLAYER 1, PLAYER 2, and PLAYER 3. There is one empty chair. Two TV trays hold snacks and drinks. They are between hands.*

PLAYER 1 (*to Jenson*): Where's our sixth tonight? Sloat have something

better to do?
> *Jenson shakes his head, then shrugs.*

PLAYER 2: So how's it looking for him? He's up for renewal, right?
CHAIR: Okay, for the most part, though there is one sticking point.
PLAYER 2: He's smart. He should.
CHAIR: Smart enough. Let's hope.
SLOAT (O.S.): Hey everybody.
PLAYER 1: Speak of the devil.
> *SLOAT enters, pulls out the empty chair.*

SLOAT: Sorry I'm late.
> *He tosses a folded twenty-dollar bill at Jenson before sitting down. Jenson slides over to him the customary stacks of chips.*

CHAIR: Are we playing here or what? (*To Player 2*) Your deal.
> *Player 2 collects the cards and starts to shuffle. Later. A hand ends. Sloat has more chips than he started with. He rakes in a modest pot, then stands.*

SLOAT: I need a break.
> *He leaves.*

SLOAT (O.S., CONT'D): Won't be long!
PLAYER 2: Hear about that librarian who took a header off the roof of UC?
> *Everybody nods.*

PLAYER 2 (CONT'D): I haven't heard a thing since the President's email.
PLAYER 3: I heard it was suicide.
PLAYER 1: I heard accidental. I take it she liked going out there to smoke—cigarettes, of all things.
CHAIR: It may have been something more sinister. At the last admins meeting, they said police detectives were interviewing everyone on the library payroll.
PLAYER 2: I wonder if it'll ever come out.
> *Sloat returns and sits down.*

SLOAT: What's the game?
> *Player 3 starts shuffling. Later. A game of hold 'em is in process, a sizable pot in the middle. The face-up cards, all hearts, are the ace, ten, king, and queen. Only the river is face-down.*

CHAIR: So, John, have you given any more thought to my advice? Everyone at this table believes in consensus significance. You meet with the committee tomorrow. I hope you're with us on this. I hope you're

on board.
PLAYER 2: Hey, Sloat, you knew that Devyn what's-her-name, didn't you?
*Sloat loses focus, speaking as if from a distance...*
SLOAT: Gail. Devyn Gail.

FLASHBACK: EXT. UNIVERSITY COLLEGE – ROOF – NIGHT
*SLOAT stands close to the edge of the roof with his back to it. DEVYN stands opposite, the open window behind her, facing him. He turns his head to the side and back, a half headshake. His mouth forms the word "No". Her eyes go wide, her face contorting. Her feet begin to lunge forward at him, arms wild. Her right arm lifts as she approaches. Sloat's eyes narrow. His right foot moves forward and turns inward 45 degrees.*
END FLASHBACK

*Sloat's eyes are intense, then soften. We pull back to reveal him sitting at the poker table.*
CHAIR: So, are you on board? Can I count on you?
PLAYER 1: Are we playing here or what? Bet's to Sloat.
*Sloat looks at Player 1, then the Chair, then straight ahead. He speaks without moving and to no one in particular...*
SLOAT: I'm all in.
*We back away from the table slowly.*

EXT. UNIVERSITY COLLEGE – DAY
*We move toward the main entrance. The weather is fine. We hear BIRDSONG and STUDENTS enjoying the beautiful day. But no one can be seen. As we approach nearer, something on the pavement on the right draws our attention. It is a police outline of a body lying not perpendicular but parallel to the side of the building. No bloodstains are visible. The cheerful sounds continue as we slowly...*

FADE OUT

<u>THE END</u>

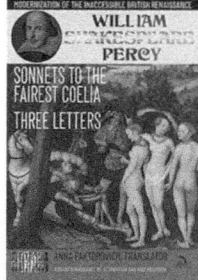

# BRRAM

## 20-Volume Series

Proves with computational linguistics, handwriting and biographical analysis:

## 6 GHOSTWRITERS

Created All British Renaissance Texts

First translations of inaccessible books, with annotations, introductions

**https://AnaphoraLiterary .com/Attribution**

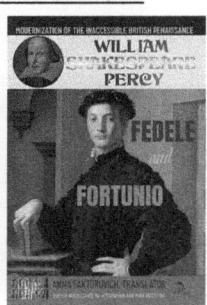

www.ingramcontent.com/pod-product-compliance
Lightning Source LLC
Chambersburg PA
CBHW031217090426
42736CB00009B/952